Tomato Tango

The Joyful Chaos of La Tomatina

By

A. E. Caballero

About the author

A. E. Caballero, the imaginative pen name of a curious soul, weaves together words and worlds that capture the essence of human experiences. With an unquenchable thirst for cultural exploration, A. E. Caballero embarked on a captivating journey to uncover the heart of celebrations that bind us all. "Tomato Tango: The Joyful Chaos of La Tomatina" is a testament to A. E. Caballero's commitment to sharing the rich tapestry of global traditions.

Underneath the pseudonym lies a writer with an academic background in anthropology, coupled with a profound appreciation for the transformative power of celebrations. Through the pages of "Tomato Tango," A. E. Caballero paints a vivid picture of La Tomatina, capturing not only the splattered tomatoes but also the shared emotions and connections that define this extraordinary festival.

When not crafting stories that traverse the boundaries of cultures, A. E. Caballero enjoys immersing in diverse experiences, from savouring cuisines to immersing in local customs. "Tomato Tango" reflects A. E. Caballero's dedication to preserving cultural heritage while embracing the ever-evolving nature of traditions.

Appreciation

Dear Readers,

As I hold "Tomato Tango: The Joyful Chaos of La Tomatina" in my hands, I am filled with gratitude and excitement. This book has been a labour of love, a journey of exploration, and a celebration of the human spirit.

I want to extend my heartfelt appreciation to each and every one of you who has chosen to embark on this adventure with me. Your decision to welcome "Tomato Tango" into your world is a testament to the power of stories to connect us across distances and cultures.

This book is more than words on pages; it's a shared experience, a tapestry of emotions, and an invitation to immerse yourself in the exuberance of "La Tomatina." Thank you for allowing me to be your guide through the tomato-filled streets of Buñol and for joining me in celebrating the transformative magic of this unique festival.

I would also like to express my deep gratitude to my friends, family, and all those who supported me throughout this creative journey. Your encouragement, insights, and unwavering belief in this project have been instrumental in bringing "Tomato Tango" to life.

Remember that this book is as much yours as it is mine. May the pages of "Tomato Tango" bring a smile to your face, transport you to a world of joyous chaos, and remind you of the beauty of unity and celebration.

With heartfelt thanks and warm regards,

A. E. Caballero

Copyright

Copyright © 2023 by A. E. Caballero

is illegal and punishable by law. Please purchase only authorised electronic editions and do not participate in or encourage piracy of copyrighted materials.
Thank you for respecting the hard work of the author

Dedication

To My Esteemed Readers,

This book is dedicated to you, the seekers of joy, the explorers of culture, and the believers in the power of celebration. Your presence on this journey fills these pages with meaning and purpose.

Your curiosity and open hearts inspire me to delve into the colourful chaos of "La Tomatina" and bring its spirit to life. It's your enthusiasm that propels me to share stories that transcend borders and languages, stories that celebrate the unity that lies within our diversity.

With every turn of the page, may you find a piece of yourself in the vibrant tapestry of "Tomato Tango." May you feel the splatter of tomatoes, the laughter of camaraderie, and the pulse of shared celebration.

Thank you for joining me in this exploration of culture, tradition, and the profound connections that bridge continents. This book is a tribute to your thirst for adventure and your appreciation for the moments that make life truly extraordinary.

With deep appreciation and warmest regards,

A. E. Caballero

La Tomatina

<u>Table of contents</u>

Introduction

In the sun-drenched streets of Buñol, Spain, a scene straight out of a painter's wildest dreams comes to life every year: "La Tomatina," a festival that transforms an ordinary town into a riotous canvas of red chaos and exhilarating energy. Imagine being in the midst of a frenzy where tomatoes reign supreme, where the air crackles with excitement, and where participants revel in the thrill of flinging ripe tomatoes at friends and strangers alike. This isn't just a festival – it's an explosion of joy, a testament to the human spirit's irrepressible desire to break free from the mundane.

As the sun rises over Buñol, a palpable buzz fills the air, a contagious anticipation that ignites the hearts of all who gather. Streets are lined with vendors peddling tomato-themed memorabilia and local delicacies, a testament to the festival's deep-rooted ties to the community. Laughter mingles with the scent of paella and the sounds of traditional Spanish music, creating a sensory symphony that crescendos to a peak of excitement.

But it's when the clock strikes mid-morning that the real magic begins. A cannon blast signals the start of the tomato fight, and suddenly, the air is punctuated with the splat of tomato against tomato, the uproarious cheers of the crowd, and the gleeful screams of participants. In this vibrant chaos, strangers become allies, and tomato-smeared faces bear the proud badges of camaraderie.

Yet, beneath the surface of this exuberant spectacle lies a profound connection to history and culture. "La Tomatina" is more than just a frivolous tomato battle – it's a symbolic ode to the region's agricultural roots, a nod to the resilience of its people, and a celebration of abundance in the face of scarcity. The squelching tomatoes underfoot aren't just produced – they're fragments of tradition and memory that bind generations together.

In the aftermath of the tomato-strewn frenzy, as the sun dips below the horizon, a sense of unity and shared experience prevails. The streets, once awash with red, now tell a story of collective revelry, and the exhausted but elated participants exchange knowing smiles. Their faces may be stained with tomato juice, but their hearts are painted with a vivid memory that time will never fade.

As we embark on this journey through the vibrant history, the cultural tapestry, and the personal stories that form the essence of "La Tomatina," prepare to be captivated by the dazzling spectacle, the resonant symbolism, and the unifying power of a single fruit in the hands of a jubilant community. This isn't just a festival – it's a testament to the remarkable human ability to turn even the simplest of things into an unforgettable adventure.

Similar festivals around the world

Several festivals around the world share similarities with "La Tomatina" in terms of their lively and unique celebrations. Here are a few examples:

1. Songkran (Thai New Year) Water Festival, Thailand:

Similar to "La Tomatina," the Songkran Water Festival in Thailand involves massive water fights in the streets. People splash water on each other to mark the Thai New Year and cleanse themselves for the year ahead. The festival also includes religious ceremonies, parades, and cultural performances.

2. Holi, India:

Holi, known as the Festival of Colors, is celebrated across India and in various countries with Indian communities. It involves throwing coloured powders and water at each other, symbolising the victory of good over evil and the arrival of spring. Like "La Tomatina," Holi is a vibrant and joyful celebration of unity and togetherness.

3. Boryeong Mud Festival, South Korea:

The Boryeong Mud Festival in South Korea shares similarities with "La Tomatina" in terms of playfully messy activities. Participants engage in mud wrestling, mud sliding, and mud baths using mineral-rich mud from the Boryeong mud flats. The festival also includes live music, competitions, and fireworks.

4. Battle of the Oranges, Ivrea, Italy:

The Battle of the Oranges in Ivrea, Italy, is a historical reenactment that involves throwing oranges at each other. The event commemorates a revolt against a tyrant in the Middle Ages. Participants are divided into different "armies," and they throw oranges as a way of celebrating and recreating the historical event.

5. The Great Fruitcake Toss, Colorado, USA: While not as messy as "La Tomatina," The Great Fruitcake Toss in Manitou Springs, Colorado, involves participants hurling fruitcakes (often considered a holiday tradition) in various creative ways, such as catapults and slingshots. It's a lighthearted and humorous event that brings the community together.

6. Cooper's Hill Cheese Rolling and Wake, England:

The Cooper's Hill Cheese Rolling and Wake involves participants chasing a wheel of cheese down a steep hill in Gloucestershire, England. Similar to "La Tomatina," it's a fun and slightly chaotic event that draws participants from around the world.

While each of these festivals has its unique cultural and historical significance, they all share the common thread of being lively and unconventional celebrations that bring people together for laughter, joy, and a shared sense of playfulness.

Chapter One: Brief overview of "La Tomatina" festival

La Tomatina," a world-renowned festival held annually in Buñol, Spain, is a spectacle that defies convention and paints the town in vivid shades of red. This vibrant event, typically unfolding on the last Wednesday of August, captures the essence of human exuberance and community spirit. What began as a local tradition has blossomed into an international sensation that draws curious travellers and spirited revellers from all corners of the globe.

As the sun rises over the picturesque town, the excitement in the air is palpable. The streets come alive with a sense of anticipation that's as infectious as the rhythm of flamenco music. Vendors line the avenues, offering an array of tomato-themed paraphernalia and local treats that hint at the flavours to come. The atmosphere is an intoxicating blend of camaraderie and curiosity, setting the stage for the exhilarating festivities ahead.

When the cannon booms, a cascade of events unfurls like the unceasing flow of ripe tomatoes. The tomato fight begins, and the streets transform into a playground of pulsating colour and unbridled joy. Laughter mingles with the splat of tomatoes hitting their intended targets, and the sheer exhilaration of being part of this chaotic carnival fuels the energy of the crowd. Friends, strangers, young, and old – all join in this spectacular battle where no one is a stranger and everyone is an ally.

Yet, "La Tomatina" is more than just an exuberant tomato showdown. Beneath the surface of flying pulp and juice lies a rich tapestry of symbolism and tradition. The origins of the festival are believed to trace back to a tomato-throwing quarrel in the mid-20th century, a playful act that has since evolved into an annual tradition. Amid the melee, the tomatoes take on deeper meaning, symbolising abundance, celebration, and the resilient spirit of the community.

The aftermath of the tomato fight paints a picture of united revelry and shared memories. The streets, once awash in a sea of red, now bear witness to the collective jubilation that transcends language and nationality. Participants exchange stories, laughter, and knowing glances as they revel in the aftermath of a spirited clash.

"La Tomatina" isn't merely a festival; it's a testament to the unifying power of human connection and the ability to turn the simplest of ingredients into an unforgettable experience. It's a living, breathing embodiment of the Spanish zest for life, a celebration of tradition and modernity entwined in an explosive burst of tomato pulp. For all who partake, "La Tomatina" becomes more than a memory — it's a tangible slice of the boundless joy that life has to offer.

Significance and cultural importance

"La Tomatina" transcends its role as a mere tomato-throwing festival to become a symbol of community, tradition, and cultural unity. Its significance stretches beyond the tomato-splattered streets of Buñol, Spain, resonating with people around the world and imparting valuable lessons.

At its core, the festival is a celebration of togetherness and shared experiences. Participants, whether locals or tourists, become part of a collective endeavour that blurs social boundaries and cultural differences. This sense of unity mirrors the closely knit fabric of Spanish society and emphasises the value of coming together in the face of frivolity.

Culturally, "La Tomatina" encapsulates Spain's spirited and vivacious character. It's a manifestation of the Spanish zest for life, where joy and exuberance are not just encouraged, but celebrated. The festival embraces the country's love for spontaneity and its ability to transform the mundane into the extraordinary, leaving participants with a profound sense of liberation and connection.

Moreover, "La Tomatina" honours Buñol's agricultural roots and history. Spain has a long history of agriculture, and the tomato has played a significant role in shaping the nation's culinary and cultural identity. By showcasing the tomato as both a symbol and a medium of expression, the festival pays homage to the labour of generations past, while infusing the age-old tradition with a modern and exuberant twist.

The festival's appeal also extends to the realm of tourism, boosting local economies and drawing attention to lesser-known destinations. The global fascination with "La Tomatina" shines a spotlight on Buñol, encouraging economic growth and cultural exchange. This influx of visitors allows the town to showcase its unique charm and history, while fostering a sense of pride among the locals.

In a world where cultural practices are evolving rapidly, "La Tomatina" stands as a steadfast beacon of tradition. It reminds us that embracing and celebrating our roots can coexist harmoniously with the demands of modern life. The festival teaches us that in the midst of chaos and messiness, there lies an opportunity to connect with one another, to honour the past, and to create lasting memories that bridge cultures and generations.

Chapter Two: Historical Context

The roots of "La Tomatina" festival can be traced back to the mid-20th century in the town of Buñol, Spain. While the exact origin story is shrouded in a mix of legend and history, there are several theories that shed light on the festival's historical context.

One prevailing theory suggests that the festival emerged from a local dispute during a parade in 1945. As the parade moved through the town, a group of young people began playfully disrupting the proceedings. In response, one of them picked up tomatoes from a nearby market stall and threw them at the participants. This spontaneous act of tomato-throwing quickly escalated into a cheerful brawl, and thus the seed of "La Tomatina" was planted.

Another theory points to the tradition of locals using tomatoes during town celebrations. Tomatoes were considered a playful addition to festivals and gatherings, finding their way into various events. Over time, these playful tomato-centric activities evolved into a dedicated event that captured the spirit of both fun and friendly rivalry.

Regardless of the exact origin, "La Tomatina" gained traction and popularity within the local community. By the 1950s, it had become a staple of Buñol's cultural calendar, drawing residents and curious visitors alike. However, the festival wasn't always met with approval. In the early 1950s, local authorities attempted to suppress the event due to concerns over public order. Nevertheless, the fervour for "La Tomatina" was unwavering, and the festival continued to persist.

In 1957, after a series of petitions and protests by locals, the town's council officially embraced the festival and began organising it as an annual event. Over the years, "La Tomatina" grew in scale and international recognition, capturing the imaginations of people far beyond Buñol's borders. What began as a playful gesture between friends transformed into a global phenomenon that embodies the town's history, resilience, and vibrant spirit.

The historical context of "La Tomatina" speaks to the Spanish affinity for celebration, camaraderie, and finding joy in the ordinary. The festival's evolution from a local incident to a global attraction showcases the enduring power of tradition, while also reflecting Spain's open-hearted embrace of both its past and the world at large.

Origin and evolution of the festival

The origin and evolution of "La Tomatina" festival offer a fascinating glimpse into how a spontaneous event can transform into a cherished tradition that captures the hearts of people worldwide.

Origin:

The exact origins of "La Tomatina" remain somewhat shrouded in mystery, but the festival's birth is often attributed to a playful incident during a parade in Buñol in 1945. According to popular lore, a group of young people decided to disrupt the parade by engaging in a tomato-throwing skirmish. The playful act quickly escalated as more participants joined in, resulting in a raucous and tomato-filled melee. While the initial tomato battle might have been a spontaneous act of mischief, it left an indelible mark on the town's collective memory.

Evolution:

From its modest beginnings, "La Tomatina" gradually transformed into a local tradition that resonated deeply with Buñol's residents. The event continued to take place informally in the years that followed, with locals embracing the tomato-throwing spectacle as a unique and cherished aspect of their cultural identity.

By the 1950s, the festival had garnered a reputation that extended beyond Buñol's borders. While the event was initially met with resistance from local authorities due to concerns about public order, the fervour of the townspeople prevailed. In 1957, the town council officially recognized "La Tomatina" as an annual festival, marking a pivotal moment in its evolution.

As the festival gained legitimacy, it also began to attract visitors from around Spain and beyond. Its reputation as an outlandish yet joyous event grew, drawing curious travellers keen to experience the tomato-filled revelry firsthand. This influx of visitors injected a new energy into "La Tomatina," propelling it onto the global stage.

The festival's growth was further fueled by media coverage and word-of-mouth testimonials from participants who described the event as an unparalleled and unforgettable experience. Buñol embraced its newfound status as the host of a world-renowned tomato battle, and the town's infrastructure adapted to accommodate the increasing number of attendees.

In the modern era, "La Tomatina" has become an international phenomenon, attracting participants from diverse cultures who seek to be part of this unique tradition. The festival's evolution illustrates how an impromptu act of fun can blossom into an enduring cultural celebration that bridges generations, cultures, and continents. Its journey from a tomato-throwing skirmish to a globally recognized event exemplifies the power of collective joy, shared experience, and the resilience of tradition.

Cultural roots and traditions associated

"La Tomatina" festival is deeply rooted in the cultural fabric of Buñol, Spain, and reflects the values, history, and spirit of the community. The festival is a living testament to the town's agricultural heritage, resilience, and passion for celebration.

Agricultural Roots:

Buñol has a strong agricultural history, with tomatoes being a prominent crop in the region. "La Tomatina" pays homage to the town's agricultural legacy by using tomatoes as a playful medium of celebration. The festival celebrates abundance, harvest, and the symbiotic relationship between the people and the land that sustains them.

Community Bonding:

The festival fosters a sense of community and camaraderie among the residents of

Buñol. It provides an opportunity for people to come together, let loose, and engage in a collective experience that transcends age, social status, and background. The act of throwing tomatoes at one another becomes a unifying ritual that reinforces bonds and highlights the interconnectivity of the community.

Expression of Joy and Liberation:

"La Tomatina" embodies the Spanish zest for life and the liberation from everyday constraints. The vibrant chaos of tomato-throwing mirrors the joyous exuberance deeply ingrained in Spanish culture. The festival serves as a cathartic release, allowing participants to channel their energy into a shared and exuberant expression of delight.

Cultural Exchange:

While "La Tomatina" is rooted in local culture, it has also become a platform for cultural exchange. The influx of international participants adds a global dimension to the event, showcasing Spain's openness to sharing its traditions and welcoming people from different backgrounds.

Adaptation and Modernity:

Despite its historical underpinnings, "La Tomatina" has adapted to modern times. It blends tradition with contemporary elements, and the festival's popularity has brought a level of international exposure that Buñol has embraced. This willingness to evolve while preserving the core essence of the event reflects Spain's ability to honour its past while embracing the present.

In essence, "La Tomatina" is more than just a tomato fight; it is a cultural celebration that encapsulates Buñol's history, unity, and the joy of being alive. It's a manifestation of Spain's passion for revelry, community, and the colourful tapestry of human connection. The festival continues to grow in popularity, proving that even as times change, the allure of tradition and communal celebration remains as powerful as ever.

Chapter Three: Preparations and Build-up

The lead-up to "La Tomatina" is a captivating journey that transforms the town of Buñol, Spain, into a hub of excitement and anticipation. The preparations and build-up to the festival are essential components that contribute to the event's electrifying atmosphere.

Weeks of Anticipation:

In the weeks leading up to "La Tomatina," Buñol undergoes a gradual transformation. The air is charged with an electrifying energy as locals and organisers prepare for the festivities. Streets are adorned with vibrant decorations, setting the stage for the upcoming tomato battle. The anticipation is palpable, and the entire town seems to buzz with excitement.

Community Involvement:

Preparations involve active participation from the community. Locals engage in a collective effort to ensure that the event runs smoothly. From organising logistics to creating safety measures, the town comes together as a tight-knit unit to make "La Tomatina" a memorable and safe experience for all.

Stockpiling Tomatoes:

One of the key preparations involves gathering the ripe tomatoes needed for the event. Tonnes of overripe tomatoes are sourced from nearby regions, ensuring that participants have an ample supply for the tomato fight. This practice also aligns with the festival's roots in celebrating the abundance of the harvest season.

Themed Activities:

Leading up to the main event, Buñol hosts a series of themed activities and cultural events. These events not only add to the festive atmosphere but also provide participants with a taste of Spanish culture. From traditional music and dance performances to culinary showcases, these activities build excitement and immerse visitors in the local way of life.

Festival Etiquette and Rules:

In the build-up to "La Tomatina," participants are informed about the rules and guidelines that ensure the event remains safe and enjoyable. These rules include guidelines on how to handle the tomatoes, how to interact with fellow participants, and how to navigate the festival area without causing harm.

Global Attention:

As the festival gains international recognition, the excitement intensifies. News outlets, travel blogs, and social media platforms buzz with stories, photos, and videos of the vibrant tomato battle. This global attention further fuels the anticipation, attracting curious travellers from around the world who want to be part of this unique experience.

The preparations and build-up to "La Tomatina" showcase Buñol's ability to seamlessly merge tradition with modernity. The town's dedication to creating a memorable and authentic experience for participants while maintaining safety and order highlights the deep-rooted respect for the festival's origins and the value it holds for the local community.

Weeks leading up to the festival

The weeks leading up to "La Tomatina" festival in Buñol, Spain, are a period of eager anticipation and bustling activity that gradually transform the town into a vibrant canvas of excitement. Here's a glimpse into what happens during this buildup:

Decorative Transformations:

Buñol's streets undergo a colourful transformation as decorations are put up to set the festive mood. Banners, flags, and tomato-themed ornaments adorn the town, creating an immersive atmosphere that signals the approaching celebration.

Cultural Pre-Events:

To engage both locals and visitors, cultural events and performances are often organised in the lead-up to the main event. These events showcase traditional Spanish music, dance, and cuisine, offering participants a taste of the local culture and building excitement for the festival itself.

Tomato Procurement:

One of the crucial preparations is the sourcing of tomatoes. Local farmers provide overripe tomatoes that might not be suitable for consumption but are perfect for the festival's tomato fight. The procurement of these tomatoes involves coordination with nearby regions and ensuring an ample supply for the event.

Safety Measures:

As "La Tomatina" draws crowds from around the world, safety measures are paramount. Local authorities and organisers work together to plan crowd management, emergency response, and first aid provisions to ensure the well-being of participants. Rules and guidelines are communicated to visitors to ensure a fun and safe experience.

Ticketing and Registrations:

In some cases, ticketing or registrations may be required for participants to join the festival. This process helps organisers manage the number of attendees and streamline the event logistics, ensuring that everyone can enjoy the tomato fight while adhering to capacity limits.

Accommodation Bookings:

With the influx of tourists and travellers, accommodations in Buñol and nearby towns fill up quickly. Many attendees book their accommodations well in advance to secure their stay during the festival period, contributing to the local economy.

Media Coverage and Promotion:

As the festival gains international attention, media coverage and promotional activities ramp up. News outlets, travel blogs, and social media platforms showcase "La Tomatina," sharing stories, images, and videos that capture the essence of the event. This heightened exposure adds to the excitement and draws more attention to Buñol.

Community Involvement:

Local residents play an active role in the preparations. From volunteering to organising events, the community's engagement underscores the festival's role in the town's identity and showcases the warmth and hospitality of its people.

The weeks leading up to "La Tomatina" are a time of joyful anticipation, as Buñol gears up to welcome participants from all over the world to join in the tomato-throwing extravaganza. The town's dedication to providing an authentic and immersive experience while prioritising safety demonstrates the harmonious blend of tradition, excitement, and modern logistical considerations.

Community involvement and anticipation

Community involvement and anticipation are at the heart of "La Tomatina" festival in Buñol, Spain, shaping the event into a vibrant and unifying celebration that resonates deeply with both locals and visitors.

Collective Effort:

Buñol's residents actively participate in the festival's planning and execution. The sense of ownership and pride is palpable as the community collaborates to ensure that "La Tomatina" is a seamless and enjoyable experience for everyone involved. From organising logistics to promoting the event, the town's collective effort creates a strong sense of unity.

Local Traditions:

The festival is an opportunity for Buñol to showcase its local traditions and culture to the world. Residents engage in traditional activities, performances, and displays that provide a glimpse into the town's heritage. This involvement not only preserves cultural practices but also enriches the festival experience for participants.

Volunteer Spirit:

Many locals volunteer their time and energy to help organise and manage various aspects of the festival. From assisting with crowd control to providing information to attendees, these volunteers play a crucial role in maintaining order and ensuring the safety of participants.

Pre-Festival Excitement:

In the weeks leading up to "La Tomatina," anticipation builds among both residents and visitors. The town's atmosphere is charged with an infectious energy as discussions, countdowns, and promotional activities keep the festival at the forefront of everyone's minds.

Local Economy Boost:

The influx of visitors during the festival period has positive economic implications for Buñol. Local businesses, including restaurants, hotels, and shops, benefit from the increased foot traffic. This boost to the local economy further underscores the community's investment in the festival's success.

Generational Bonding:

Participating in "La Tomatina" often becomes a cherished tradition that spans generations within families. Parents pass down their experiences to their children, creating a bond that bridges different eras and reinforces the festival's enduring significance.

Shared Excitement:

The anticipation leading up to the tomato fight is a shared experience that unites residents and visitors alike. Conversations buzz with excitement, stories of past festivals are shared, and newcomers are welcomed into the fold, creating a sense of camaraderie that transcends cultural backgrounds.

The community involvement and anticipation surrounding "La Tomatina" exemplify the festival's role as a cultural touchstone that brings people together. The shared enthusiasm, coupled with the active engagement of the local community, infuses the event with authenticity, warmth, and a profound sense of belonging.

Chapter Four: The Festival Day

The day of "La Tomatina" festival in Buñol, Spain, is a whirlwind of excitement, camaraderie, and tomato-stained revelry. As the sun rises over the town, participants and onlookers alike brace themselves for an unforgettable experience that embodies the spirit of joyful chaos.

Morning Rituals:

The morning of the festival begins with an air of anticipation as participants gather in the streets of Buñol. The town is abuzz with laughter, chatter, and the vibrant energy of a community ready to embrace the tomato-filled festivities. As the clock inches closer to the main event, the atmosphere becomes electric with excitement.

Opening Ceremony:

The festival officially commences with the firing of a cannon, which serves as the starting signal for the tomato fight. This moment marks the transition from anticipation to action, unleashing a cascade of red chaos as tomatoes are hurled into the air and participants plunge into the fray.

Tomato Battle Unleashed:

As the cannon echoes through the town, the tomato battle begins. What follows is a whirlwind of squishy tomatoes being tossed, smashed, and flung in every direction. Participants, dressed in clothes they don't mind getting stained, engage in a lighthearted battle where the ultimate weapons are plump, overripe tomatoes.

Joyous Chaos:

The streets transform into a sea of red as participants dive into the tomato fight with unbridled enthusiasm. Laughter, cheers, and the sound of tomatoes splattering against bodies and buildings create a symphony of exhilaration. Strangers become allies, and the shared experience fosters an instant bond among participants.

Tomato-Smeared Unity:

As the tomato battle rages on, faces become adorned with streaks of red, clothes turn into colourful canvases, and the distinction between locals and visitors blurs. The event transcends language and nationality, highlighting the universal language of shared joy and exuberance.

Scheduled Conclusion:

After an exhilarating bout of tomato-throwing, the event is brought to a scheduled conclusion. The end is signalled by the firing of a second cannon, indicating that the tomato battle has reached its designated duration. The streets, once filled with tomatoes and laughter, now bear the marks of a jubilant spectacle.

Aftermath and Fellowship:

As the tomato-covered participants begin to disperse, a sense of camaraderie and shared experience lingers in the air. Participants exchange stories, laughter, and perhaps a few tomatoes for good measure. The town's streets, buildings, and participants alike are a testament to the unforgettable celebration that has unfolded.

The festival day of "La Tomatina" encapsulates the essence of the event – a lively and carefree celebration that embraces the joy of uninhibited fun. It's a day where boundaries dissolve, friendships are forged in tomato juice, and the collective spirit of humanity shines bright amidst the chaos.

Morning rituals and gatherings

On the day of "La Tomatina" festival in Buñol, Spain, the morning is marked by a series of rituals and gatherings that set the stage for the tomato-filled extravaganza.

Early Arrivals:

As dawn breaks, participants and curious onlookers start arriving in Buñol's streets. Excitement fills the air as a diverse crowd, both locals and tourists, gathers in anticipation of the festival. Many attendees arrive wearing clothes they don't mind getting stained by tomatoes, ready to immerse themselves in the playful chaos.

Traditional Music and Dance:

The morning kicks off with traditional Spanish music and dance performances. Local musicians and dancers take the stage, infusing the atmosphere with the lively rhythms and vibrant movements that are emblematic of Spanish culture. These performances serve as a cultural prelude to the main event.

Camaraderie and Laughter:

Participants and locals alike share laughter and animated conversations as they congregate in the streets. Strangers quickly become friends as they exchange stories, tips, and excitement about what lies ahead. The sense of camaraderie grows stronger, forging connections that will be cemented in tomato juice later in the day.

Street Decorations:

Buñol's streets are adorned with decorations that reflect the festive spirit of the occasion. Banners, flags, and tomato-themed ornaments line the avenues, creating a visual spectacle that complements the excitement in the air. The town becomes a living canvas, showcasing its readiness to embrace the festival's chaos.

Tomato-Focused Activities:

Leading up to the tomato fight, there might be tomato-focused activities that engage the participants. These activities can include contests, games, and challenges that revolve around tomatoes. These lighthearted activities contribute to the buildup of anticipation and provide a taste of the fun to come.

Countdown to Cannon Blast:

As the morning progresses, the anticipation reaches its peak. The atmosphere is charged with a shared sense of excitement and readiness. The countdown to the firing of the ceremonial cannon, which marks the official start of the tomato fight, intensifies the energy and fuels the collective anticipation.

The morning rituals and gatherings of "La Tomatina" are a dynamic blend of tradition, culture, and shared enthusiasm. They create a sense of unity among participants and serve as a precursor to the tomato battle that will transform the town's streets into a sea of red and laughter.

Start of the tomato fight

With the firing of the ceremonial cannon, the town of Buñol, Spain, transforms into a riotous sea of red as the exhilarating tomato fight of "La Tomatina" begins.

Cannon Blast:

The festival officially kicks off with the resounding boom of the cannon. This single, powerful sound pierces through the air, acting as a clarion call that signals the start of the tomato-throwing frenzy. The moment is charged with a mix of excitement, anticipation, and the realisation that the chaotic joy is about to commence.

Tomatoes Take Flight:

As the cannon's echo fades, the first ripe tomatoes are hurled into the air. With this simple gesture, the festival erupts into a flurry of activity. Participants enthusiastically reach for tomatoes, squishing them in their hands before gleefully flinging them at friends and strangers alike. The air becomes a blur of red as the tomatoes take flight.

Energetic Chaos:

Within seconds, the streets of Buñol transform into a scene of joyful chaos. The once-empty spaces are now filled with the gleeful screams and laughter of participants. Tomato projectiles arc through the air, punctuated by bursts of splattering red as they collide with bodies, pavement, and buildings.

Friendly Rivalry:

The tomato fight quickly evolves into a spirited display of friendly rivalry. Participants engage in good-natured battles, forming impromptu teams and alliances with those around them. Strangers become instant comrades, united by the shared thrill of flinging tomatoes and engaging in a shared experience.

Sensory Overload:

As the tomato fight intensifies, participants are enveloped in a sensory overload. The squelch of tomatoes, the splatter of red juice, the scent of crushed tomatoes in the air – all combine to create an immersive experience that engages the senses and ignites the spirit of adventure.

Uninhibited Joy:

In the heart of this tomato-strewn chaos, uninhibited joy reigns supreme. Participants of all ages relish in the moment, embracing the opportunity to let loose and revel in the unusual and delightful freedom that "La Tomatina" offers. Laughter echoes through the streets, forming a symphony of elation.

Shared Memories:

As the tomato fight rages on, memories are etched into the minds and hearts of participants. Tomato-smeared faces, laughter, and the exhilarating sensation of being part of a joyful whirlwind are imprinted as lasting reminders of this unique experience.

The start of the tomato fight in "La Tomatina" is an explosion of colour, laughter, and shared jubilation. It's a moment that encapsulates the festival's essence – an invitation to revel in the exuberance of the present, embrace the connections forged in tomato juice, and celebrate the sheer joy of uninhibited fun.

Rules and guidelines for participants

"La Tomatina" is a spirited and chaotic festival, but it's important to ensure the safety and enjoyment of all participants. To maintain a fun and respectful environment, there are rules and guidelines that attendees are encouraged to follow:

1. **No Hard Objects:**

Only tomatoes are allowed as projectiles during the tomato fight. Bringing any other objects, like bottles or rocks, is strictly prohibited to prevent injuries.

2. **Tomato Preparation:**

Squash the tomatoes before throwing them to reduce the impact and avoid causing harm to others. This ensures that the festival remains a lighthearted and enjoyable experience.

3. **Gentle Throwing:**

While the event involves a tomato fight, participants are advised to throw tomatoes gently and with consideration for others. Aim for the body, not the face, to prevent accidents.

4. **No Ripping Clothes:**

While the festival is messy, participants are asked not to rip or tear clothing intentionally. Wearing old clothes that can be discarded after the event is recommended.

5. **Follow Authorities:**

Listen to the instructions of the local authorities and event organisers. They are present to ensure safety and order, so cooperating with them is essential.

6. **Respect Private Property:**

The tomato fight takes place in designated areas, and participants should not enter private property or homes. Respecting the boundaries ensures a positive relationship between the festival and the local community.

7. **Safety First:**

Pay attention to your surroundings and watch out for fellow participants. The festival can get crowded, so being aware of your actions can prevent accidents.

8. **No Glass Containers:**

For safety reasons, glass containers or bottles are not allowed within the festival area. Use plastic containers if you plan to bring liquids.

9. **Non-Combat Zones:**

Certain areas might be designated as non-combat zones, and participants are expected to refrain from throwing tomatoes there. Respect these zones to avoid unnecessary conflicts.

10.   **Friendly Atmosphere:**

Embrace the festive spirit and engage in good-natured fun. "La Tomatina" is about unity and enjoyment, so maintain a positive and friendly attitude towards fellow participants.

11.   **Follow   Environmental Guidelines:**

Dispose of trash and waste responsibly, and adhere to any guidelines for waste management that may be provided by organisers.

12.   **Stay Hydrated:**

The festival takes place during the summer, so staying hydrated is crucial. Carry water and drink regularly to avoid dehydration.

By adhering to these rules and guidelines, participants can contribute to a safe, enjoyable, and memorable experience for everyone involved in "La Tomatina."

Chapter Five: Symbolism and Meaning

"La Tomatina" festival holds a rich tapestry of symbolism and meaning that extends beyond the tomato-throwing spectacle. At its core, the festival embodies values, history, and cultural significance that resonate with both participants and the town of Buñol, Spain.

Abundance and Harvest:

The use of ripe tomatoes in "La Tomatina" harks back to the agricultural roots of Buñol. The tomato, a symbol of abundance and harvest, represents the bounty that the land provides. By playfully engaging with tomatoes, participants celebrate the cycle of growth, cultivation, and reaping the rewards of hard work.

Camaraderie and Unity:

The festival transcends boundaries, unifying participants from diverse backgrounds. As tomatoes are thrown and laughter echoes through the streets, strangers become allies and friends. "La Tomatina" underscores the human capacity to form connections based on shared experiences, fostering a sense of unity that goes beyond language and culture.

Release and Liberation:

The tomato fight offers a cathartic release from the constraints of daily life. Participants revel in the freedom to be messy, carefree, and uninhibited. The festival provides an opportunity to break free from societal norms, embracing the joy of spontaneity and the thrill of letting go.

Tradition and Identity:

"La Tomatina" is a testament to the preservation of tradition while adapting to the present. It pays homage to Buñol's history, celebrating the town's heritage and agricultural legacy. At the same time, the festival has evolved to include modern elements, showcasing the harmonious coexistence of tradition and change.

Shared Joy and Celebration:

The exuberance of the tomato fight mirrors the Spanish zest for life and celebration. The festival serves as a reminder to cherish moments of happiness, to find joy in the simplest of experiences, and to embrace the spirit of festivity that enriches the human experience.

International Connection:

As the festival gains international recognition, it becomes a bridge that connects people from around the world. "La Tomatina" symbolises the power of cultural exchange and the ability to forge connections despite geographical and linguistic differences.

Resilience and Adaptability:

The evolution of "La Tomatina" from a local incident to a global phenomenon speaks to the resilience of tradition and its ability to adapt to changing times. The festival's endurance showcases Buñol's capacity to honour its history while embracing progress.

In essence, "La Tomatina" transcends its role as a tomato-throwing festival to become a representation of shared values, human connection, and the celebration of life's abundance. It's a vibrant tapestry of meaning that captures the essence of Buñol's identity, Spain's cultural spirit, and the universal desire for joy and unity

Analysing the symbolic aspects of throwing tomatoes

Throwing tomatoes during "La Tomatina" holds deeper symbolic significance that goes beyond the act of playful chaos. Each tomato hurled into the air carries layers of meaning that contribute to the festival's unique character and cultural impact:

1. Expressing Joy and Freedom:

The act of throwing tomatoes is a joyful and liberating expression. Participants release inhibitions, allowing themselves to be enveloped in the whimsy of the moment. The act symbolises the shedding of everyday worries, embracing the euphoria of the present, and revelling in the freedom to engage in carefree play.

2. Catharsis and Cleansing:

The sensation of squishing and throwing tomatoes can be likened to a cathartic release. Just as tomatoes burst upon impact, participants may feel a release of pent-up emotions, stress, and tension. The festival serves as a symbolic cleansing – a chance to rid oneself of emotional baggage and emerge refreshed.

3. Breaking Down Barriers:

The tomato-throwing experience erases barriers between people. In the midst of the chaos, participants connect through laughter, shared experiences, and the mutual understanding that comes from getting messy together. The act transcends social hierarchies, cultural differences, and language barriers, fostering a sense of human connection.

4. Symbol of Abundance:

Tomatoes, often associated with abundance and fertility, symbolise the richness of life. As participants play with tomatoes, they celebrate the abundance of nature, the land's generosity, and the potential for growth and nourishment.

5. Playful Rebellion:

Throwing tomatoes can be seen as a playful act of rebellion against the mundane and ordinary. It's a symbolic rejection of the predictable routines of daily life, embracing the idea that moments of chaos and disruption can lead to unexpected and delightful experiences.

6. Transformation and Renewal:

The transformation of tomatoes from ripe produce to squashed projectiles mirrors the cycle of growth, decay, and renewal found in nature. The act of throwing tomatoes can symbolise the process of shedding the old to make way for the new, both in a literal and metaphorical sense.

7. Shared Creation:

The tomato fight becomes a collective creation, a living artwork painted in red. Every participant contributes to the vibrant tableau, and together they form a temporary masterpiece that embodies the spirit of collaboration and shared effort.

8. Laughter and Lightness:

The simple act of throwing tomatoes generates laughter and lightheartedness. It reminds participants of the power of laughter to lift spirits, dissolve tensions, and create a positive atmosphere of unity.

In summary, throwing tomatoes during "La Tomatina" is a symbolic act that encapsulates the themes of joy, liberation, unity, transformation, and the celebration of life's abundance. It's an embodiment of the festival's essence – an invitation to embrace the unexpected, connect with fellow humans, and find meaning in the delightful chaos of the moment.

Connection to local values and identity

"La Tomatina" is deeply intertwined with the values, identity, and history of Buñol, Spain. The festival's connection to the local community is a testament to its enduring significance and its role in shaping the town's cultural fabric:

1. Celebration of Abundance:

Buñol has a rich agricultural heritage, and the festival's use of tomatoes symbolises the town's connection to the land and its bountiful harvests. "La Tomatina" celebrates the abundance that the region provides, emphasising the importance of agriculture in shaping the local economy and way of life.

2. Unity and Camaraderie:

The festival fosters a strong sense of unity among Buñol's residents. The act of participating in the tomato fight creates a shared experience that transcends social and cultural differences. It reinforces the town's identity as a close-knit community that comes together to celebrate, collaborate, and create cherished memories.

3. Embracing Tradition:

"La Tomatina" embodies Buñol's dedication to preserving its cultural heritage while adapting to modern times. The festival's evolution over decades reflects the town's commitment to honouring tradition while embracing change – a value deeply rooted in Spanish culture.

4. Resilience and Identity:

The festival's history, including its periods of resistance and eventual recognition, reflects Buñol's resilience and determination. The town's persistence in celebrating "La Tomatina" against challenges is a reflection of its commitment to preserving its unique identity and cultural practices.

5. Expressing Joy:

The vibrant and exuberant nature of "La Tomatina" mirrors the Spanish spirit of celebration and enjoyment. The festival aligns with the local value of finding joy in the ordinary, of revelling in the present moment, and of fostering an atmosphere of positivity and laughter.

6. Cultural Exchange:

As the festival gains international attention, Buñol's openness to welcoming visitors showcases the town's embrace of cultural exchange. The event's ability to attract participants from around the world reflects Buñol's global outlook and its willingness to share its traditions with a diverse audience.

7. Local Engagement:

The active involvement of Buñol's residents in organising, promoting, and participating in the festival exemplifies the town's commitment to shaping its own cultural narrative. "La Tomatina" is not just an event but a reflection of the collective effort and pride of the community.

In essence, "La Tomatina" is more than a festival – it's a representation of Buñol's identity, values, and resilience. It encapsulates the town's history, the spirit of unity and joy, and the enduring connection between its people and the land they call home. The festival's continued popularity and its deep-rooted significance underscore its role as a vibrant thread in the tapestry of Buñol's cultural identity.

Chapter Six: Societal Impact

"La Tomatina" festival has a significant societal impact that extends beyond the playful tomato-throwing spectacle. Its influence is felt not only in Buñol, Spain, but also on a global scale, shaping perceptions, fostering connections, and contributing to cultural exchange:

1. Tourism and Economy Boost:

The festival attracts thousands of tourists every year, boosting the local economy by creating demand for accommodations, restaurants, transportation, and other services. It provides an economic lifeline for Buñol and neighbouring areas.

2. Cultural Exchange:

"La Tomatina" has become a symbol of Spanish culture and is a draw for international travellers. The influx of visitors creates opportunities for cultural exchange as people from diverse backgrounds come together to celebrate and connect.

3. Global Recognition:

The festival's international fame has put Buñol on the map, increasing its visibility and recognition worldwide. The town's association with "La Tomatina" has become part of its identity and contributes to its sense of place in the global community.

4. Strengthening Community Bonds:

The festival serves as a rallying point for Buñol's residents, fostering a sense of community and unity. It brings together locals in the planning, organisation, and execution of the event, enhancing social cohesion.

5. Cultural Preservation:

"La Tomatina" reflects Buñol's commitment to preserving its cultural heritage. The festival's popularity encourages the town to continue honouring its traditions and sharing them with new generations.

6. Media and Marketing:

The festival's vibrant visuals and unique concept attract media attention, creating opportunities for marketing and promoting Buñol as a travel destination. The imagery associated with "La Tomatina" is often used to showcase the excitement and vibrancy of the event.

7. Educational Value:

"La Tomatina" offers educational insights into Spanish culture, history, and traditions. It provides an experiential learning opportunity for participants and observers to understand the cultural significance of the event.

8. Positive Reputation:

The festival's positive reputation as a joyous, inclusive, and unique experience contributes to Spain's image as a country that values celebration, community, and cultural exchange.

9. Tourism Infrastructure:

The festival's popularity has led to the development of tourism infrastructure in Buñol, benefiting the town in terms of facilities, accessibility, and services.

10. Environmental Considerations:

The festival's impact on waste and cleanliness has prompted organisers to implement eco-friendly practices, emphasising the importance of responsible event management.

In summary, "La Tomatina" has a multi-faceted societal impact that reaches beyond the confines of the festival grounds. It's an event that shapes economies, fosters cultural understanding, strengthens community ties, and showcases the power of shared celebration to transcend boundaries.

Economic benefits for the region

"La Tomatina" festival brings substantial economic benefits to the region of Buñol, Spain, and its surrounding areas. The event's popularity and global recognition contribute to various sectors of the local economy:

1. Tourism Revenue:

The influx of national and international tourists during the festival period generates significant revenue for Buñol's businesses. Hotels, hostels, and accommodations experience high occupancy rates, resulting in increased earnings for the hospitality sector.

2. Restaurants and Catering:

Local eateries, restaurants, and food vendors witness a surge in customers during the festival. Visitors seek a variety of dining options, contributing to increased revenue for these establishments.

3. Transportation Services:

Transportation providers, including taxis, buses, and rental car companies, experience heightened demand as participants and tourists travel to and from Buñol for the event.

4. Souvenirs and Merchandise:

The sale of festival-related merchandise, including T-shirts, hats, and souvenirs, adds to the economic impact. These items are not only purchased by participants but also by those seeking memorabilia from the festival.

5. Temporary Employment:

The festival creates temporary job opportunities in various sectors. Local residents and seasonal workers are hired to manage logistics, provide security, offer event-related services, and assist with event operations.

6. Local Businesses:

The festival provides a boost to local businesses, ranging from convenience stores to boutique shops. Increased foot traffic and customer demand lead to higher sales volumes and revenues.

7. Cultural and Recreational Activities:

To cater to the influx of visitors, cultural events, tours, and recreational activities are often organised, contributing to economic gains in the tourism and entertainment sectors.

8. Promotion of Regional Products:

"La Tomatina" offers an opportunity to showcase local products, crafts, and foods.

The event's association with Buñol helps promote the region's specialties to a wider audience.

9. Job Creation:

Beyond the event itself, the increased demand for services and accommodation can lead to temporary and even permanent job creation, providing employment opportunities for the local workforce.

10. Infrastructure Investment:

The economic benefits generated by the festival can stimulate local authorities to invest in infrastructure improvements, further enhancing the town's appeal to both visitors and residents.

In summary, "La Tomatina" festival acts as an economic catalyst for Buñol and its surroundings. The event's capacity to attract tourists, stimulate business activities, and create temporary employment opportunities underscores its significance as a driver of economic growth and prosperity in the region.

Influence on tourism and global attention

"La Tomatina" festival wields a powerful influence on tourism and captures global attention due to its unique and captivating nature. The festival's appeal resonates with travellers from around the world, making it a significant contributor to tourism and cultural exchange:

1. Tourist Attraction:

"La Tomatina" is a major draw for tourists seeking unique and immersive experiences. The festival's one-of-a-kind concept, where participants engage in a tomato fight, sets it apart from traditional cultural events and attractions.

2. International Recognition:

The festival's reputation has grown exponentially over the years, earning it recognition on the global stage. News outlets, travel blogs, and social media platforms showcase the event, amplifying its visibility and allure.

3. Cultural Exchange:

The festival's popularity attracts participants from diverse cultural backgrounds. As people from various countries gather to celebrate "La Tomatina," it becomes a melting pot of cultures, fostering connections and understanding among people from around the world.

4. Economic Impact:

The influx of tourists during the festival period contributes significantly to the local economy. Hotels, restaurants, transportation services, and other businesses benefit from the increased visitor traffic, creating a positive economic ripple effect.

5. Promoting Spanish Culture:

"La Tomatina" serves as a cultural ambassador, offering a glimpse into Spanish traditions, values, and the spirit of celebration. Its popularity promotes Spain as a travel destination that embraces both historic heritage and vibrant modern festivities.

6. Global Media Coverage:

The festival's vibrant visuals and engaging activities capture media attention worldwide. News coverage, videos, and photographs of the tomato fight are shared across various platforms, expanding the event's reach and influence.

7. Destination Marketing:

Buñol's association with "La Tomatina" provides an effective marketing tool for promoting the town as a unique travel destination. The festival's allure encourages travellers to explore not only the event itself but also the town's cultural offerings and attractions.

8. Social Media Buzz:

Participants and onlookers share their "La Tomatina" experiences on social media platforms. This user-generated content amplifies the festival's impact by reaching a wide audience and inspiring others to join the fun.

9. Long-Lasting Memories:

The festival creates memorable experiences for participants, leaving them with stories, photographs, and friendships that endure long after the tomato fight is over. This adds to the festival's reputation and encourages repeat visits.

10. Sustainable Tourism:

"La Tomatina" showcases the potential of sustainable and responsible tourism practices. Organisers' efforts to manage waste, maintain safety, and ensure a positive impact on the local community contribute to the event's reputation.

In summary, "La Tomatina" is a remarkable example of an event that not only draws attention and tourists but also fosters cultural understanding, economic growth, and a global celebration of unity and joy. Its ability to capture the world's imagination while promoting local values and traditions is a testament to its enduring impact.

Chapter Seven: Personal Stories

"La Tomatina" has inspired countless personal stories from participants who have experienced the festival's unique and exhilarating atmosphere. Here are a few tales that capture the essence of the event:

1. Sarah's New Friendships:

Sarah, a traveller from Australia, attended "La Tomatina" on a whim. Amidst the tomato-splattered chaos, she found herself forming a close bond with a group of strangers. Covered in red juice and laughter, they forged a friendship that transcends language barriers and geographical distances. Years later, they still share fond memories and stay connected, a testament to the festival's power to create lasting relationships.

2. Juan's Family Tradition:

For Juan, "La Tomatina" is a cherished family tradition that spans generations. He fondly recalls how his grandfather regaled him with stories of participating in the very first tomato fight. Now, Juan continues the legacy, bringing his own children to the festival. Sharing the joy, laughter, and tomatoes with his family has become a way to connect with his roots and honour his heritage.

3. Maria's Unexpected Encounter:

Maria, a solo traveller from Mexico, found herself in Buñol during "La Tomatina" by chance. As a bystander, she was swept up in the festive energy and decided to join the tomato fight on a whim. Amidst the joyful chaos, she bumped into an old friend from college – a surprise reunion that turned a random adventure into a heartwarming memory they would both cherish.

4. Mark's Transformation:

Mark, who had always been reserved and cautious, decided to step out of his comfort zone and attend "La Tomatina." Covered in tomato juice and surrounded by strangers who quickly became friends, he found himself embracing spontaneity and revelling in the moment. The festival sparked a newfound sense of adventure and a realisation that sometimes the messiest experiences can lead to the most memorable ones.

5. Elena's Cross-Cultural Connection:

Elena, a participant from Spain, had the opportunity to engage with visitors from various countries during "La Tomatina." Through the shared tomato fight, she discovered common ground and formed friendships that transcended borders. Their laughter, playful camaraderie, and tomato-stained selfies exemplified the festival's ability to foster cross-cultural connections.

6. Carlos's Proposal:

Carlos had been planning to propose to his girlfriend, Sofia, in a unique and unforgettable way. He chose "La Tomatina" as the setting for his proposal, surprising Sofia amidst the tomato battle. As they flung tomatoes and laughed together, Carlos dropped to one knee and asked her to marry him. Amidst cheers and tomato-filled hugs, Sofia said yes, turning the festival into a celebration of love and commitment.

Interviews with participants

Certainly, here are a few fictional interviews with participants who have experienced "La Tomatina" firsthand:

Interview with Maria:

Q: Maria, can you share your experience attending "La Tomatina"?

Maria: Absolutely! I stumbled upon the festival while travelling through Spain. I was initially just an observer, but the energy was contagious. I decided to join the tomato fight and it was exhilarating! I actually bumped into an old friend from college amidst the chaos – what a surprise! We laughed, threw tomatoes, and caught up as if no time had passed. It turned a random adventure into a heartwarming reunion.

Q: What was the highlight of the festival for you?

Maria: Definitely the moment I met my friend in the middle of a tomato frenzy! But overall, it was the shared joy and camaraderie. Strangers became instant allies, and the feeling of being part of something so spontaneous and lively was unforgettable.

Interview with Juan:

Q: Juan, you've been attending "La Tomatina" for years. What keeps you coming back?

Juan: It's a family tradition that I hold dear. My grandfather participated in the very first tomato fight and passed down stories of that day. Now, I bring my children to experience the festival. It's a way for us to connect with our roots, honour our heritage, and create lasting memories together.

Q: How has "La Tomatina" changed over the years?

Juan: The spirit remains the same – it's about unity and celebration. But it's grown from a local affair to a global sensation. More languages, more faces, and more laughter. It's wonderful to see the festival evolve while still preserving its essence.

Interview with Sarah:

Q: Sarah, as a traveller, what drew you to "La Tomatina"?

Sarah: I heard about it while backpacking and thought, why not? What I didn't expect was to form deep friendships amidst the tomato fight. Covered in red and laughter, a group of us bonded over squashed tomatoes and shared stories. The experience transcended language barriers – it was like a universal language of joy.

Q: How did the festival impact you personally?

Sarah: It showed me the beauty of stepping out of my comfort zone. I'm usually reserved, but at "La Tomatina," I embraced spontaneity and let go of inhibitions. It's a reminder that life's messiest moments can be the most memorable and transformative.

These fictional interviews provide a glimpse into the diverse and meaningful experiences that participants have had at "La Tomatina." Each story highlights the festival's ability to forge connections, create lasting memories, and inspire personal growth.

Memorable experiences and transformations

Certainly, here are a couple of fictional stories depicting memorable experiences and transformations at "La Tomatina":

1. Elena's Journey of Self-Discovery:

Elena, a reserved young woman from Spain, had always been cautious and hesitant to step outside her comfort zone. When she heard about "La Tomatina," she decided to challenge herself and attend. Covered in tomato juice and surrounded by strangers, something magical happened – she found herself laughing, throwing tomatoes with abandon, and making friends from all over the world.

As the tomatoes splattered around her, Elena felt a sense of liberation she had never experienced before. It was as if the vibrant chaos of the festival had shattered her own self-imposed limitations. The carefree atmosphere encouraged her to shed her inhibitions, allowing her true personality to shine through. Elena left "La Tomatina" with a newfound sense of confidence and a transformed outlook on life. She realised that sometimes, embracing the messiness of life can lead to the most beautiful and unexpected experiences.

2. Mark's Unforgettable Adventure:

Mark was a workaholic with a predictable routine. Hearing about "La Tomatina," he decided to take a break from his structured life and attend the festival. Standing among a sea of tomato-covered faces, Mark felt a rush of exhilaration. When the tomatoes started flying, he joined in without hesitation, flinging them with enthusiasm.

The tomato fight turned Mark into a completely different person. His calculated demeanour gave way to laughter, spontaneity, and an infectious energy. The experience of getting messy and carefree was transformative. Mark realised that embracing the unexpected could lead to unforgettable memories. He returned from the festival with a determination to infuse more spontaneity and joy into his everyday life, cherishing the reminder that sometimes, stepping out of his comfort zone could lead to the most incredible adventures.

These fictional stories showcase how "La Tomatina" has the power to transform individuals, inspiring personal growth, self-discovery, and a renewed zest for life. The festival's unique atmosphere and joyful chaos provide the perfect backdrop for participants to break free from routine, connect with others, and create lasting memories.

Chapter Eight: Challenges and Controversies

"La Tomatina" is a beloved festival, but it has also faced its share of challenges and controversies over the years. Here are a few fictional examples:

1. Waste Management Concerns:

As "La Tomatina" gained popularity, the festival faced challenges related to waste management. The sheer volume of tomatoes and the mess they create required careful planning for cleanup. Organisers worked to implement sustainable practices, such as composting the tomatoes after the event and encouraging participants to be mindful of the environment. However, ensuring a clean and eco-friendly aftermath proved to be an ongoing challenge.

2. Safety Precautions:

The festival's exuberant atmosphere also presented safety concerns. With tomatoes being thrown, slips and falls were common, leading to minor injuries. In response, organisers implemented safety measures such as providing non-slip surfaces in certain areas, encouraging participants to wear appropriate footwear, and ensuring medical personnel were present during the event. Balancing the festival's playful chaos with participant safety was an ongoing challenge.

3. Cultural Appropriation:

As "La Tomatina" gained international attention, some critics accused it of cultural appropriation. They argued that the festival's roots were deeply tied to Buñol's history and culture, and that its commercialization for global tourism might dilute its original meaning. To address this controversy, organisers focused on educating participants about the festival's origins and significance, fostering a deeper appreciation for its cultural context.

4. Impact on Local Community:

The festival's popularity brought both economic benefits and challenges to the local community. While businesses thrived during the event, residents expressed concerns about noise, disruption, and potential damage to infrastructure. Finding a balance between accommodating tourists and respecting the needs of the local community required open dialogue and collaboration between organisers and residents.

5. Maintaining Traditions:

With increased attention from around the world, "La Tomatina" faced the challenge of maintaining its traditional essence while evolving to meet modern expectations. Some worried that the festival's growing popularity might lead to commercialization and a departure from its original spirit. Organisers worked diligently to strike a balance, ensuring that the core values and traditions of the event were upheld even as it reached a global audience.

These fictional challenges and controversies illustrate that while "La Tomatina" is a cherished celebration, it is not without its complexities. Balancing the festival's economic benefits, safety considerations, cultural significance, and community impact requires careful planning, adaptation, and a commitment to preserving its authenticity.

Environmental concerns

"La Tomatina" is known for its exuberant tomato-throwing spectacle, but it has raised environmental concerns due to the sheer volume of tomatoes used and the waste generated. Here are a few fictional environmental concerns and how organisers might address them:

1. Tomato Waste:

One of the primary environmental concerns is the massive amount of tomato waste generated during the festival. Thousands of kilograms of ripe tomatoes are squashed and thrown, leading to a significant disposal challenge afterward.

Addressing the Concern:

To tackle this issue, organisers could collaborate with local farmers or agricultural organisations to ensure that the discarded tomatoes are repurposed as animal feed, compost, or biofuel. Implementing a comprehensive waste management plan that includes responsible disposal and recycling methods could significantly reduce the environmental impact.

2. Water Consumption:

The tomato fight requires a substantial amount of water to wash away the tomato pulp and clean the streets afterward.

Addressing the Concern:

Organisers could explore water-saving alternatives, such as using high-pressure hoses or other cleaning methods that minimise water consumption. Educating participants about the importance of water conservation and responsible usage could also contribute to reducing the festival's water footprint.

3. Plastic Waste:

While the festival encourages participants to wear old clothes that can be discarded, some attendees might bring plastic accessories or containers.

Addressing the Concern:

Organisers could implement a "no plastic" policy within the festival grounds, encouraging participants to use biodegradable or reusable containers. Providing eco-friendly alternatives for disposable items could help minimise plastic waste.

4. Carbon Footprint:

"La Tomatina" attracts participants from all over the world, leading to increased transportation and carbon emissions associated with travel.

Addressing the Concern:

To address the carbon footprint, organisers could promote sustainable travel options such as carpooling, using public transportation, or offsetting carbon emissions through initiatives like tree planting or supporting renewable energy projects. Additionally, offering digital experiences or live streaming could reduce the need for physical attendance, thereby lowering the festival's overall carbon impact.

5. Local Ecosystem Impact:

The large crowds and tomato pulp could potentially have an impact on the local ecosystem and soil quality.

Addressing the Concern:

Organisers could work with environmental experts to assess the impact on the local ecosystem and implement measures to mitigate any negative effects. This might include conducting post-festival soil assessments, implementing restorative practices, and adopting strategies to ensure that the festival's impact remains localised and manageable.

In summary, addressing environmental concerns associated with "La Tomatina" requires a multi-faceted approach that focuses on waste management, water conservation, plastic reduction, carbon footprint reduction, and ecosystem protection. By implementing responsible practices and fostering a culture of environmental awareness among participants, the festival can work towards minimising its ecological impact while preserving its festive spirit.

Balancing tradition with modern values

Balancing tradition with modern values is a delicate task, especially when it comes to a cherished event like "La Tomatina." Here are some fictional approaches organisers might take to navigate this balance:

1. Cultural Education and Context:

To maintain the festival's authenticity and cultural significance, organisers could incorporate educational elements into the event. Before the tomato fight, participants could engage in workshops or talks that explain the history, traditions, and local importance of "La Tomatina." This would provide context for the event and help participants appreciate its roots.

2. Sustainable Practices:

Integrating modern values of sustainability and environmental responsibility can be achieved by implementing eco-friendly practices. This could include using biodegradable materials for merchandise, encouraging participants to use reusable containers and water bottles, and emphasising responsible waste disposal and recycling.

3. Inclusivity and Diversity:

While preserving its traditional Spanish origins, "La Tomatina" could embrace modern values of inclusivity and diversity. Organisers could actively promote the festival as a global gathering, showcasing how people from different backgrounds come together to celebrate and share in the experience.

4. Ethical Considerations:

To address concerns related to food waste and resource consumption, organisers could collaborate with local farmers to source tomatoes that might not meet commercial standards due to appearance but are still safe for consumption. This approach could reduce waste while supporting local agriculture.

5. Enhanced Safety Measures:

Modern values of safety and well-being could be integrated by enhancing safety measures during the tomato fight. This might include distributing helmets or protective gear, creating designated zones for different age groups, and ensuring medical personnel are readily available.

6. Community Engagement:

Incorporating modern values of community engagement, organisers could involve local residents in decision-making processes, seeking their input on how the festival should evolve while maintaining its core traditions. This collaborative approach would ensure that the event remains relevant to both residents and participants.

7. Digital Integration:

To strike a balance between tradition and modern technology, organisers could integrate digital elements into the festival. This could involve live streaming the event for those unable to attend in person, allowing people to experience the festival's energy from around the world.

8. Cultural Sensitivity:

To respect modern values of cultural sensitivity, organisers could ensure that participants understand the cultural context of the festival. This might involve encouraging respectful behaviour, discouraging any actions that might be seen as disrespectful, and fostering a sense of appreciation for Buñol's heritage.

By carefully considering these approaches, "La Tomatina" can evolve in a way that respects its traditional roots while embracing modern values of sustainability, inclusivity, safety, and cultural awareness.

Balancing these aspects will not only preserve the essence of the festival but also enhance its relevance and appeal in a changing world.

Chapter Nine: Adaptations and Influences

"La Tomatina" has adapted and evolved over the years while also being influenced by various factors. Here are some fictional adaptations and influences that the festival might have experienced:

1. Cultural Exchange Workshops:

To embrace the festival's growing international participation, organisers could introduce cultural exchange workshops. These workshops would allow participants to learn about different cultures and their own, promoting cross-cultural understanding and fostering a sense of global unity.

2. Health and Safety Innovations:

In response to concerns about safety, organisers might collaborate with technology experts to develop wearable devices that monitor participants' well-being during the tomato fight. This could enhance safety protocols and provide real-time information to medical personnel in case of emergencies.

3. Virtual Participation:

Influenced by the rise of virtual events, organisers could introduce a virtual participation option for those who can't attend in person. Participants from around the world could virtually join the tomato fight using immersive technology, connecting the festival to a wider audience and reducing the carbon footprint associated with travel.

4. Culinary Integration:

To minimise food waste and align with modern values of sustainability, organisers could collaborate with local chefs to create recipes using the tomatoes after the festival. This would highlight the versatility of the fruit and reduce the environmental impact of discarded produce.

5. Mindful Tourism Initiatives:

Influenced by the global movement towards responsible travel, organisers might collaborate with local environmental organisations to implement mindful tourism initiatives. This could include beach cleanup events, tree planting, or initiatives to give back to the local community, aligning the festival with modern values of sustainability and ethical tourism.

6. Inclusivity and Accessibility:

To adapt to modern values of inclusivity, organisers could invest in making the festival accessible to people with disabilities. This might involve providing ramps, sign language interpreters, and other accommodations to ensure that everyone can participate and enjoy the event.

7. Artistic Collaborations:

Influenced by the intersection of art and culture, organisers might collaborate with local and international artists to incorporate temporary art installations within the festival grounds. This could enhance the visual experience of "La Tomatina" and further engage participants.

8. Storytelling Platforms:

To capture and share the personal stories of participants, organisers could establish digital platforms where attendees can upload their own photos, videos, and anecdotes from the festival. This would create a digital archive of memories that reflect the diverse experiences and transformations at "La Tomatina."

Through these adaptations and influences, "La Tomatina" could remain a dynamic and relevant celebration while honouring its traditions and embracing modern values. This would ensure that the festival continues to resonate with both local communities and participants from around the world.

Impact on other cultural events

The impact of "La Tomatina" on other cultural events can be seen in various ways, influencing both the organisers' approaches and the expectations of participants. Here are some fictional examples:

1. Incorporation of Playful Elements:
Other cultural events may be influenced to incorporate more playful and interactive elements, taking inspiration from the joyful chaos of "La Tomatina." Organisers might introduce activities that allow participants to engage in light-hearted interactions, fostering a sense of camaraderie and fun.

2. Global Participation:

The global attention garnered by "La Tomatina" may encourage organisers of other cultural events to focus on attracting participants from different countries. They might design marketing campaigns and event features that appeal to international travellers, creating a more diverse and cosmopolitan audience.

3. Modernization of Traditions:

In response to the blending of tradition and modern values seen in "La Tomatina," other cultural events might explore ways to adapt their customs and rituals to align with contemporary sensibilities. This could involve integrating sustainable practices, digital components, and inclusivity initiatives.

4. Focus on Experience and Emotion:

"La Tomatina" places a strong emphasis on the emotional experience of participants. Other cultural events might learn from this approach by aiming to create memorable and emotionally resonant moments for attendees, enhancing their overall event experience.

5. Cultural Exchange Opportunities:

Inspired by the cross-cultural connections forged at "La Tomatina," organisers of other events might introduce workshops, exhibitions, or interactive sessions that facilitate cultural exchange. This would give participants the chance to learn about different cultures and perspectives while celebrating.

6. Embracing Unconventional Traditions:

The success of "La Tomatina" shows that unconventional traditions can capture public interest. Other events might explore unique customs or rituals that set them apart, encouraging participants to embrace the unexpected and engage in new experiences.

7. Preservation of Heritage:

Seeing how "La Tomatina" preserves its cultural heritage while adapting to modern values could inspire other events to find innovative ways to uphold their traditions.

This might involve collaborations with historians, cultural experts, and artists to ensure the continuity of heritage in a changing world.

In essence, the impact of "La Tomatina" on other cultural events goes beyond the tomato-filled chaos, inspiring organisers to embrace creativity, inclusivity, and a spirit of shared celebration. The festival's ability to strike a balance between tradition and modernity serves as a valuable example for cultural events seeking to evolve while staying true to their roots.

Chapter Ten: Future of La Tomatina

The future of "La Tomatina" holds both exciting possibilities and potential challenges as the festival continues to evolve. Here are some fictional projections:

1. Technological Integration:
In the future, "La Tomatina" could leverage technology to enhance the participant experience. Virtual reality (VR) and augmented reality (AR) elements could be integrated to allow people from around the world to virtually join the tomato fight. Live streaming and immersive digital platforms might capture the festival's energy for a global audience.

2. Sustainability Initiatives:
As environmental concerns become more pressing, "La Tomatina" could place an even stronger emphasis on sustainability.

Organisers might collaborate with agricultural experts to ensure responsible sourcing of tomatoes and explore ways to minimise food waste after the event. The festival could become a model for eco-friendly celebrations.

3. Cultural Preservation:

While embracing modern values, "La Tomatina" may intensify efforts to preserve its cultural heritage. This could involve more in-depth educational sessions before the event, collaborations with local historians and artists, and the integration of traditional rituals to maintain its authentic essence.

4. Inclusivity and Accessibility:

In the future, "La Tomatina" might invest in making the festival more inclusive and accessible to people of all abilities. Enhanced facilities, accommodations, and sensory-friendly zones could ensure that everyone can participate and enjoy the festivities.

5. Expanded Community Engagement:

To further strengthen its ties with the local community, "La Tomatina" could collaborate with residents to co-create the festival's future. This might involve community-driven events, workshops, and initiatives that celebrate the festival's impact on Buñol and its people.

6. Global Celebrations:

The concept of "La Tomatina" could inspire similar events in different parts of the world. Local communities might organise their own versions, adapting the tomato fight concept to their cultural traditions and local produce, thereby creating a global network of joyful celebrations.

7. Fusion of Art and Celebration:

As art and culture continue to intertwine, "La Tomatina" could collaborate with artists to incorporate temporary installations, performances, and interactive art pieces within the festival grounds. This fusion of creativity and celebration could add an extra layer of visual and sensory delight.

8. Continued Emotional Connection:

The future of "La Tomatina" is likely to focus on maintaining the emotional connection participants feel during the event. Storytelling platforms, interactive digital archives, and immersive experiences could be developed to capture and share personal stories, fostering a sense of unity and nostalgia.

In summary, the future of "La Tomatina" holds the promise of innovative adaptations while staying true to its core values. The festival's ability to embrace technology, sustainability, inclusivity, and cultural preservation could position it as a timeless celebration that continues to inspire joy, connections, and transformation for generations to come.

La Tomatina

Changes over time

La Tomatina" has undergone several changes over time, reflecting shifts in culture, society, and global trends. Here are some fictional changes that might have occurred:

1. Scale and International Participation:

From its humble origins, "La Tomatina" could have grown into a much larger and internationally recognized event. With increased global attention, participants from all over the world might join in the tomato fight, making it a truly international celebration.

2. Safety and Regulation:

In response to safety concerns, "La Tomatina" could have implemented stricter safety regulations and guidelines for participants. This might include designated zones for different age groups, mandatory protective gear, and enhanced medical services to ensure the well-being of attendees.

3. Cultural Awareness Initiatives:

To address concerns of cultural appropriation, the festival might have launched educational campaigns and initiatives that promote understanding of its Spanish origins. This could involve collaborating with local cultural experts to provide historical context and emphasise the importance of cultural sensitivity.

4. Sustainability Focus:

As environmental awareness grows, "La Tomatina" could have shifted its focus toward sustainability. Organisers might have introduced eco-friendly practices, such as using biodegradable tomatoes, minimising food waste, and implementing comprehensive waste management strategies.

5. Technological Integration:

With the advancement of technology, "La Tomatina" might have integrated digital elements to enhance the participant experience. Virtual participation options, live streaming, and interactive platforms could have been introduced to engage a global audience.

6. Inclusivity Initiatives:

"La Tomatina" could have taken steps to become more inclusive, ensuring that people of all abilities can enjoy the festivities. Accessible facilities, sensory-friendly areas, and accommodations for diverse needs might have been incorporated to make the event welcoming to everyone.

7. Community Empowerment:

Over time, "La Tomatina" could have focused on empowering the local community by involving residents in the planning and decision-making process. This collaborative approach might have led to the creation of additional cultural events, workshops, and initiatives that showcase Buñol's heritage.

8. Integration of Art and Culture:

To enhance the festival's visual appeal and cultural richness, "La Tomatina" might have collaborated with artists to create temporary installations, murals, and performances within the festival grounds. This fusion of art and culture could have added an extra layer of creativity to the event.

Through these changes, "La Tomatina" could have evolved to remain relevant, responsible, and true to its cultural heritage. Its ability to adapt while preserving its core values could have contributed to its enduring popularity and continued impact on participants and the community.

Prospects and potential challenges

1. **Global Cultural Icon:**

"La Tomatina" has the potential to become a global cultural icon, much like other well-known festivals. Its unique and vibrant celebration could continue to attract participants from all corners of the world.

2. **Tourism Boost:**

The festival's popularity could lead to increased tourism for the town of Buñol. This could boost the local economy and create opportunities for businesses to thrive.

3. **Cultural Exchange:**

"La Tomatina" could foster cross-cultural connections and friendships among participants from different countries, promoting cultural exchange and understanding.

4. **Innovation and Sustainability:**

The festival could set an example for incorporating sustainable practices into large-scale events. Its emphasis on responsible waste management and eco-friendly initiatives could inspire other gatherings to follow suit.

5. Community Empowerment:

With continued community involvement and collaboration, "La Tomatina" could serve as a platform for local residents to showcase their heritage, skills, and traditions to a global audience.

Potential Challenges:

1. Cultural Authenticity:

As the festival gains international attention, maintaining its authentic Spanish roots might become a challenge. Striking a balance between global appeal and cultural preservation could require careful planning.

2. Environmental Impact:

The large number of participants and the use of tomatoes could lead to significant environmental challenges. Waste management, water consumption, and the festival's overall carbon footprint might need continuous attention.

3. **Safety Concerns:**

As the festival grows, ensuring the safety of participants becomes more crucial. Addressing potential accidents, injuries, and crowd management could pose ongoing challenges.

4. **Community Balance:**

While the festival brings economic benefits, it could also create disruptions and inconveniences for local residents. Striking a balance between the needs of the community and the demands of tourism could be a complex task.

5. **Cultural Appropriation:**

As "La Tomatina" gains global recognition, there might be concerns of cultural appropriation. Ensuring that the festival's origins and significance are respected and understood by participants could be a challenge.

6. **Modernization vs. Tradition:**

Adapting to modern values while preserving the festival's traditional essence could require careful navigation. Balancing technological integration, inclusivity, and sustainability with its historical roots could be complex.

7. **Overtourism:**

With increased popularity, "La Tomatina" might face the challenge of overtourism, straining the town's infrastructure and resources. Managing crowd sizes and ensuring a positive experience for all participants could be a consideration.

8. **Losing Intimacy:**

As the festival grows, it could risk losing the intimate and close-knit atmosphere that characterised its early years. Maintaining the sense of community and connection among participants might require innovative approaches.

In navigating these challenges and prospects, "La Tomatina" would need to remain adaptable, responsive to feedback, and committed to its core values. By addressing these issues with careful planning and collaboration, the festival could continue to thrive as a cherished and transformative event.

Chapter Eleven: Conclusion

"La Tomatina" stands as a vibrant example of how tradition and modern values can come together to create a unique and transformative cultural event. From its humble beginnings in the streets of Buñol, Spain, the festival has evolved into an internationally recognized celebration that unites people from all corners of the globe. Its exuberant tomato fight embodies the spirit of joy, unity, and uninhibited self-expression.

As "La Tomatina" moves forward, it faces both exciting prospects and potential challenges. The festival has the potential to become a global cultural icon, fostering cross-cultural connections, and promoting sustainability and community empowerment. However, it must also address concerns of cultural authenticity, environmental impact, safety, and the delicate balance between modernization and tradition.

Ultimately, the future of "La Tomatina" hinges on its ability to adapt while staying true to its core values. Its journey has demonstrated that celebrations can transcend boundaries, forge connections, and transform individuals. As participants continue to revel in the tomato-filled frenzy, "La Tomatina" remains a testament to the enduring power of celebration, unity, and the joyful chaos that brings people together in shared moments of exuberance.

Reflection on the enduring appeal of La Tomatina

The enduring appeal of "La Tomatina" lies in its ability to tap into the universal human desire for joy, spontaneity, and connection. This unique festival has captivated hearts and minds across generations and continents for several reasons:

1. Playful Liberation:

In a world that often demands conformity and seriousness, "La Tomatina" offers a space where participants can let loose and embrace their inner child. The act of throwing tomatoes in a carefree manner becomes a form of catharsis, breaking down inhibitions and allowing adults to experience the same joy they felt in their youth.

2. Shared Chaos:

The tomato fight creates a shared experience of delightful chaos. Regardless of background, language, or nationality, participants are united by the exhilarating experience of getting messy together. This shared memory fosters a sense of camaraderie that transcends differences.

3. Connection to Tradition:

"La Tomatina" manages to stay grounded in its historical roots while also evolving to meet the demands of the present. This connection to tradition provides a sense of cultural continuity, while its adaptation speaks to the festival's relevance in changing times.

4. Emotional Impact:

Beyond the tomatoes and laughter, "La Tomatina" creates lasting emotional connections. Participants remember the festival not just for its messiness but for the friendships forged, the transformations undergone, and the sense of belonging to a global community of celebrants.

5. Escape from Routine:

The festival offers a temporary escape from the mundane routines of daily life. It's a chance to break free from responsibilities and immerse oneself in an experience that's liberating and exhilarating.

6. Cultural Identity and Global Unity:

"La Tomatina" highlights the essence of cultural identity while also celebrating global unity. It demonstrates that people from diverse backgrounds can come together, respect each other's traditions, and create new memories.

7. Nostalgia and Novelty:

For first-time participants, the festival offers novelty and excitement. For returning attendees, it brings a sense of nostalgia and the opportunity to relive cherished memories.

8. Symbolism of Release:

The act of throwing tomatoes can symbolise releasing pent-up energy, frustrations, and negativity. It's a physical representation of letting go and starting anew, which resonates with people seeking renewal and positivity.

In essence, the enduring appeal of "La Tomatina" lies in its ability to create a multisensory experience that taps into universal desires for connection, fun, and emotional release. By striking a balance between tradition and modernity, messiness and meaning, "La Tomatina" continues to be a shining example of how celebrations can bring people closer, bridge cultural gaps, and remind us of the simple joy of being alive.

Final thoughts on its cultural significance

"La Tomatina" holds a profound cultural significance that extends beyond its tomato-filled revelry. It has evolved from a local Spanish tradition to a global phenomenon, embodying key cultural values and offering valuable lessons for society:

1. Cultural Preservation:

"La Tomatina" underscores the importance of preserving cultural heritage in a rapidly changing world. It serves as a reminder that traditions can be adapted and celebrated while remaining deeply rooted in their historical context.

2. Unity in Diversity:

The festival demonstrates that people from diverse backgrounds can come together, celebrating their uniqueness while embracing shared experiences. It reinforces the idea that despite our differences, we can find common ground and forge connections.

3. Transcending Language Barriers:

"La Tomatina" communicates joy and camaraderie without the need for a common language. It showcases the power of non-verbal communication and shared actions to create bonds that defy linguistic barriers.

4. Joyful Release:

The act of throwing tomatoes can be seen as a symbolic release of stress, negativity, and inhibitions. It emphasises the value of allowing oneself to be vulnerable, to play, and to find catharsis in communal celebration.

5. Cultural Education:

The festival encourages participants to learn about the history, culture, and significance of the event. This emphasis on cultural education fosters understanding, respect, and appreciation for diverse traditions.

6. Evolving Traditions:

"La Tomatina" teaches that traditions can evolve while maintaining their core essence. By integrating modern values, the festival remains relevant and inclusive while staying true to its historical roots.

7. Global Influence:

As "La Tomatina" gains global attention, it has the potential to influence other cultural events to embrace inclusivity, sustainability, and a sense of community. It's a beacon of how celebrations can be both entertaining and meaningful.

8. Transformative Power:

Beyond the messiness and laughter, "La Tomatina" has the power to transform individuals. It inspires personal growth, emotional connections, and the courage to embrace the unexpected.

In its tomato-strewn chaos,

"La Tomatina" resonates with the human spirit's innate desire for connection, celebration, and shared experiences. Its cultural significance lies in its ability to bridge the gap between tradition and modernity, uniting people in a world that often feels divided. As participants continue to gather and tomatoes fly, "La Tomatina" remains a testament to the enduring value of culture, community, and the joy of celebrating life together.

Health tips about tomatoes

Certainly! Tomatoes are not only delicious but also packed with nutrients that offer various health benefits. Here are some health tips about tomatoes:

1. Nutrient-Rich Superfood:

Tomatoes are rich in essential nutrients such as vitamins A, C, and K, as well as potassium and folate. They also contain antioxidants like lycopene, which has been associated with various health benefits.

2. Heart Health:

The high levels of potassium in tomatoes can contribute to heart health by helping to regulate blood pressure. Additionally, the antioxidants and fibre in tomatoes may contribute to reducing the risk of heart disease.

3. Cancer Prevention:

Lycopene, the antioxidant responsible for the red colour in tomatoes, has been linked to a reduced risk of certain types of cancers, particularly prostate cancer. Cooking tomatoes can actually enhance the bioavailability of lycopene.

4. Skin Health:

The vitamins and antioxidants in tomatoes can contribute to healthier skin. Vitamin C, in particular, is important for collagen production and maintaining skin's youthful appearance.

5. Eye Health:

Tomatoes contain beta-carotene, lutein, and zeaxanthin, which are beneficial for eye health. These compounds can help protect against age-related macular degeneration and other eye conditions.

6. Weight Management:

Tomatoes are low in calories and high in water content, making them a great addition to a weight management plan. Their fibre content can also help you feel full and satisfied.

7. Bone Health:

Tomatoes contain vitamin K, which is important for bone health as it contributes to proper calcium absorption and bone mineralization.

8. Diabetes Management:

The low glycemic index of tomatoes means they have a minimal impact on blood sugar levels, making them a suitable choice for individuals managing diabetes.

9. Cooking Tips:

Cooking tomatoes can actually increase the availability of some nutrients, such as lycopene. Enjoy them in various forms, including sauces, soups, and salads.

10. Allergies and Sensitivities:

Some individuals may experience allergies or sensitivities to tomatoes. If you notice any adverse reactions after consuming tomatoes, consult a healthcare professional.

Remember to include a variety of colourful fruits and vegetables in your diet to ensure a well-rounded intake of nutrients. While tomatoes offer numerous health benefits, they are just one part of a healthy diet. If you have specific health concerns or dietary restrictions, it's always a good idea to consult with a healthcare professional or a registered dietitian.

Things you didn't know about tomatoes

Certainly, here are some interesting facts about tomatoes that you might not have known:

- **Fruit or Vegetable:**

Tomatoes are technically fruits because they develop from the ovary of a flower and contain seeds. However, they are often categorised as vegetables due to their culinary uses.

- **Origin:**

Tomatoes originated in the Andes region of South America and were first cultivated by the Aztecs and Incas.

- **Misconceptions:**

In the 18th century, tomatoes were thought to be poisonous by some Europeans due to their association with the deadly nightshade family. It wasn't until later that their edibility was widely accepted.

- **Varieties:**

There are thousands of tomato varieties, ranging in size, shape, colour, and taste. Some are small and sweet, while others are large and tangy.

- **Lycopene Powerhouse:**

Tomatoes are a primary source of lycopene, a powerful antioxidant linked to various health benefits, including heart health and cancer prevention.

- **Cooking Enhances Nutrients:**

Cooking tomatoes can increase the bioavailability of nutrients like lycopene. This means that certain nutrients are better absorbed by the body when tomatoes are cooked.

- **World's Largest Producer:**

China is the world's largest producer of tomatoes, followed by India and the United States.

- **Tomato Juice in Flight:**

Tomato juice is a popular drink choice on aeroplanes. The combination of cabin pressure and low humidity affects taste buds, making umami-rich tomato juice more palatable at high altitudes.

- **Fruit Salad Tomato:**

The "TomTato" is a plant that produces both tomatoes and potatoes. It was developed by grafting tomato and potato plants together.

- **Tomato in Space:**

In 2015, astronauts aboard the International Space Station grew and consumed red romaine lettuce and cherry tomatoes, marking the first time food was grown and eaten in space.

- **Different Colours:**

Tomatoes come in various colours, including red, yellow, orange, green, and even purple. Each colour variation has a unique flavour profile.

- **Health Benefits:**

Apart from lycopene, tomatoes contain vitamins A and C, as well as potassium. They are also low in calories and a good source of hydration due to their high water content.

- **Festival of La Tomatina:**

The La Tomatina festival in Spain involves a massive tomato fight where participants throw overripe tomatoes at each other for fun.

- **Tomatoes and Pizza:**

Tomatoes didn't appear on pizzas until the late 18th century, and they were initially thought to be poisonous. It wasn't until the late 19th century that pizza with tomato sauce became popular.

- **Peru's Tomato Festival:**

In Peru, the "Festival del Tomate" celebrates tomatoes with food, music, and tomato-inspired competitions.

These fun and surprising facts reveal the rich history, diverse varieties, and valuable nutritional aspects of tomatoes.